My Journey *with* JESUS

C.W.

ISBN 979-8-89345-858-9 (paperback)
ISBN 979-8-89345-859-6 (digital)

Christian Faith Publishing
832 Park Avenue
Meadville, PA 16335
www.christianfaithpublishing.com

Printed in the United States of America

Preface

My purpose for sharing this with you is to give you comfort. I want to provide you with hope in times of tribulation, inspire you in times of desolation, provoke thoughts of God in times of loneliness, and encourage you to love harder and live a more faithful, fruitful life. I want you to enjoy life regardless of your circumstances. Life is short. Trials and tribulations are inevitable, but if you have a relationship with God, He will always provide you with what you need when you need it. May you never lose faith in God's healing hand and never stop believing in yourself.

Jesus said, "If thou canst believe, all things are possible to him that believeth." (Mark 9:23 KJV)

Despite going through difficult times, God has consistently been a source of support and comfort for me. I am continuously grateful for His unwavering presence. I learned my most valuable lessons from my most painful experiences. My journey with God has been shaped by these experiences, which continue to impact who I am today. Through them, I have grown closer to God. Without the world I grew up in and the environment I was exposed to, I wouldn't be the woman I am now.

> In the beginning was the Word, and the Word was with God, and the Word was God. The same was in the beginning with God. (John 1:1–2 KJV)

My trials and tribulations began at a very early point in my life. For as long as I can remember, my mother brutally beat me. I can remember this happening as far back as two years old when my mother sat on top of my neck, suffocating the air from me. I remember I bit her. As a two-year-old baby, this was a pure survival instinct. I didn't know what I was doing; all I knew was that I couldn't breathe. I needed air and a way out from under her body. I know child psychologists and behavioral studies will tell you that children don't remember before age three, but I can tell you firsthand that you remember trauma when you've experienced it like this.

I suffered many cruelties at the hands of my mother. I remember she would take a hammer and smash a bunch of rocks, lay them on the floor in front of me, and I would have to kneel on them with my bare knees for hours. My knees would be bloody and sore for days. I still have scars on my knees as reminders.

I know God has always been there for me and will be there for you too. Even if it's not apparent right now, even if you think He's forgotten you, He hasn't.

When I was four years old, my birth mother, my six siblings, and I moved to California when my mother left my father in Lake Charles, Louisiana. My birth mother was French-Canadian but looked Caucasian with her pale complexion. My father was Creole, with a dark complexion. Unfortunately, it was the late 1950s, and the road from here only got more complicated.

Since we had left my father in Louisiana, it was just my mother and us kids in California. My siblings and I did not inherit our mother's fair complexion. In the 1950s and 1960s, there was plenty of racial discrimination for a woman who appeared Caucasian to be traveling with seven children who had dark complexions. I remember being ridiculed because of our mixed-race family. One of the first things I vividly recall when we got to California was someone asking my mother, "Whose little n—— kids are those?" I can't remember what she answered, but I assume she said, "Mine." I hope she said mine. I honestly don't know. It wasn't just in California where we endured this ridicule. I also remember being told to hide in a back bedroom, storage room, or shed back in Louisiana whenever a white person would visit the house. My step-grandmother also had a darker complexion, so she would have to hide with us. We were told to stay quiet and put our hands over our mouths.

In Louisiana, my grandfather had a high position in society. He was an upstanding white citizen, so God forbid anyone found out he favored darker-skinned women. It was not a widely acceptable practice to mingle among different races, and having children together seemed practically forbidden. It was tough to deal with, but I can still tell you that I thank God for everything.

Shortly after we left my father in Louisiana, my mother became heavily dependent on alcohol. This perpetuated an even bigger downhill spiral. My mother was emotionally and mentally ill. The physical, mental, and emotional abuse I endured was far beyond what any child, nay, what any human should ever have to endure. I was terrified of my mother. It has been well over forty years, and I still have scars from the physical abuse. At just five years old, I learned a horrible lesson: If you can't trust your own mother, who can you trust?

It wasn't more than three years after moving to California, and coincidentally during the Watts Riots on August 11, 1965, that all seven of us were taken away from my mother. This happened swiftly after my big brother made an emergency phone call to the police. I was gushing blood out of the back of my head from a stiletto heel that had been hurled at me in my mother's rage. It was four years before I had to see my mother again.

After the police came that day on August 11, 1965, four of my siblings were sent to live in Houston, Texas, and the remaining three of us, including me, were sent to MacLaren Hall in Los Angeles while we waited to be placed in a foster home. Two years later, I was the first of my two brothers to leave MacLaren Hall and be placed in a foster home. I was seven years old at the time. I was petrified to leave my brothers and go to an unknown place with an unknown person. I had no idea what to expect.

It's difficult to see the bigger picture when all you see is what you want, but God sees everything. Only God knows everything and shares it with us on a need-to-know basis. It's essential to embrace this knowledge as He gives it to us. There was no way for me to know that God's plan would be so divine.

When my foster mother arrived to take me from MacLaren Hall, she took me in her arms and sat me on her lap, hugged me, and told me I did not have to be afraid or worried and that she wasn't going to let anyone hurt me. Strangely enough, I believed her. I felt better. I felt safe. This was the beginning of the next eight years of my life.

My foster mother made me feel loved and welcomed me into her life as her daughter. I learned she was a Christian woman, a Pentecostal preacher. She was also an African-American woman. She had a slightly lighter complexion than mine, but we looked related. Nobody would have known she was my foster mother unless they were told. This was, of course, more acceptable to society at the time. When we went out in public, we weren't ridiculed for appearing to be different races.

I see now how God has always protected me, even through the tragedy of being abused by my mother, separated from my siblings, and being too young to understand what was happening. I see that God always had a plan.

I spent the next eight years being raised by my foster mother. These were the years I spent growing up, from a young girl to a teenager. These were impressionable years for me. My foster mother taught me to ride a bike, how to cook, and how to put on makeup, but the most valuable lesson she taught me was to rely on God and my faith above anything else. We had a fantastic relationship. Her wisdom was unmatched, and her loyalty was unwavering. She always kept her word, no matter the circumstances, and her actions spoke volumes about the depth of her character. She molded me into the person I am today. She taught me scriptures that I've held onto all my life. For example, "Peace

I leave with you, my peace I give unto you: not as the world giveth, give I unto you. Let not your heart be troubled, neither let it be afraid" (John 14:27 KJV).

She instilled in me the importance of specific values that have stayed with me throughout my life. She taught me to be strong and independent and to always trust in God. I did my best to learn from her experiences and knowledge about life and God, and through this, I realized that life's challenges can be opportunities to connect with God.

It was two years after being with my foster mother that my birth mother was awarded supervised visitation rights. I did *not* want to see her. I was still utterly terrified of her. She would send clothes or gifts to my foster mother for me, but having to see her in person was going to be a whole other story. I knew my foster mother wouldn't let anything happen to me while she was there, but I didn't feel like I needed to see my birth mother. I was still furious inside, and I had not begun to unpackage the horror I had trapped inside me. I knew these supervised visits were not for my benefit; they were for hers. The visits were an hour long but felt like eternity. I sat in the living room with my foster mother and my birth mother, tense, arms crossed, not making eye contact, and praying God would intervene and pass the hour in the blink of an eye. I have no idea what we all talked about for an hour, but I know I wasn't interested. I wanted nothing to do with these visits.

As a child, before my foster mother was in the picture, I didn't grow up having "role models." I grew up with "anti-role models." I knew who I didn't want to be like. I saw situations I would never want to be in myself and knew who I never wanted to be. This worked for me. I didn't need a picture-perfect life to realize what I wanted out of it.

Life will not always deal you a perfect hand, but that doesn't mean you can't shuffle the deck of life for a better outcome. It may require effort, determination, and perhaps some risk-taking, but with God, you can rest assured that your hand will never be a losing one. Don't be discouraged by what life deals you; instead, focus on the possibilities and opportunities to create a better future.

This is, of course, way easier said than done. When I was fifteen years old, my foster mother got a call from Social Services telling her that my birth mother was granted permission to retake custody of me. We were told that she had wholly given her life over to Jesus. At this time, five of my other siblings were already eighteen years old. It was only me and my younger brother, who was with a different foster family, who were minors. Unfortunately, this was not great news to me. It had been eight years, and I was still terrified of my mother. I did not want to leave my foster mother. I had a good thing going there; I felt loved, safe, and like God had placed me there to help me recover from the distrust and abuse I suffered. I felt like He gave me an environment to thrive in and be nurtured in, and now it was all being torn apart! And why? Because my birth mother said that she gave her life to Jesus? I couldn't understand why I had to leave. Just because someone says they gave their life to Jesus doesn't mean they won't make mistakes. It didn't mean she wouldn't return to her abusive ways. The suffering and fear I experienced far surpassed my trust in being reunited with my birth mother. I was only fifteen though; what could I do? So my younger brother and I were sent to live with our birth mother again, and that was that.

I do remember my birth mother apologizing to me for the physical and mental abuse I suffered, which is more than I can say for many children who were and are abused. I don't know if children often get apologies from their parents, but it's essential to know that even if you don't get the apology you feel you deserve, you can overcome it. I accepted her apology to be polite but also because I still didn't trust her.

I desperately wanted to return to my foster mother. I spent as little time at home as possible. My brother and I would run away to an abandoned train car and sit for hours. We did that on several occasions until one time, the abandoned train car wasn't so abandoned after all. It started moving! We had to jump off of it. It was funny later, but needless to say, we never did that again. I would even fake illnesses so I could go to the hospital instead of having to stay home. I was wise enough to know that if a person acts crazy enough, they get sent to a facility where they are held for at least seventy-two hours. I would have fits and lose my mind just long enough to be picked up by an ambulance and taken to a facility for troubled minors. I remember one time I got to stay in a facility for a month. Once the seventy-two hours expired, I confessed to a nurse that I didn't want to go home. The nurse told an officer working there, and the officer looked up my file. He saw that I had been previously taken away from my mother and put in a foster home. The officer told me and the nurse that I didn't have to go home if I didn't want to. Hallelujah! I was thrilled. I knew I couldn't stay there forever or even until I turned eighteen. I knew, eventually, I'd have to go home to my birth mother. So I sucked up as much time there as I could, and one month later, I was faced with having to go home.

For the next two and a half years, I was biding my time at my birth mother's house until I turned eighteen. At fifteen and a half, I had no plan for what I'd do once I turned eighteen; I only knew that legally, I did not have to stay.

As God would have it, when I turned eighteen, my birth mother and I got into an argument. Apparently, she felt as though my coming of age at eighteen meant that I was ready to date older men who would, in turn, pay my way through life. Mind you, this older man she wanted me to date was, at minimum, twice my age. He consistently flaunted around in a long, robe-like coat even during the scorching summers when it must have been unbearable underneath. He coupled this ugly coat with peculiar hats that coordinated with the ugliness of his coat. He strolled with the aid of a cane, which made me think that maybe he was even older than twice my age. My birth mother explained to me that since I had turned eighteen, I needed to think about how I was going to make a living, and a man would provide for me. I wish I had asked her how her man, my dad, worked out providing for her. However, at eighteen and still scared of her, the quip didn't even cross my mind. She said I had no place in her house if I wasn't willing to date this man and get his money. I took this argument as a fantastic opportunity, and I knew my place was nowhere in her home.

I knew where my mother kept her money, and I waited for her to leave the house that night. I went back inside, and I took her money. I walked to the gas station nearby, where I knew the owner, and I told him I needed to call the bus station and get a bus ticket. He asked me where I was going and why I was leaving so late at night. I told him everything. He told me it wasn't the safest time of night to travel and that he would call his wife to let her know he'd be home late. He told me to wait right where I was. After ending the call with his wife, he informed me that there was a room inside the gas station where I could spend the night and leave the following morning to catch the bus. He even gave me money. He said if I couldn't get on the bus, I would take a taxi to where I was going. That was the last time I ever saw him. I now understand the meaning: some people will come into your life as a blessing; others will come into your life as a lesson. Either way, no one comes into your life by accident.

I took the Greyhound bus to my foster mother's house the next morning. I recall that morning as if it were yesterday. The bus dropped me off about a half mile from where she lived. As I headed toward her house, I could see the kitchen window from the distance. I could see her standing there washing dishes, and then she saw me coming down the street. The excitement on her face is one of the best gifts I've ever received. She dropped everything and ran out of the house in her bathrobe and slippers. She came outside, opened her arms wide, and engulfed me in her loving embrace. She cried out, "My baby!" As she held onto and hugged me, she felt my sigh of relief and knew I was exhausted. That was the most loving hug I had felt in over two and a half years. My foster mother walked me inside and told the kids there to clear my room for me so I could sleep. I immediately felt "home." I slept for hours! When I woke, she fed me, and we had a long talk. I told her everything! I was so happy to be home. Being there with her this time felt different. I didn't think I could feel even more safe with her than I had before, but I did. I wasn't worried about being taken away or concerned the police were going to force me back to my birth mother's house. I was an adult now. I didn't have to leave if I didn't want to.

I got to stay with my foster mother for the next six months. During that time, she helped me establish a steady income, and she helped me apply to college. I accomplished more in those six months with my foster mother than I did in two and a half years with my birth mother. Those six months were a catalyst, setting me on a path that would shape the rest of my life.

I moved to San Diego to start college at San Diego State University at eighteen years old. I stayed in a hotel for a few nights until I found an apartment about forty-five minutes from campus. I would take the Greyhound bus to school every day, and during my commute, I met quite a few characters. I met someone I became romantically interested in, and we started dating. He was a United

States Marine. We dated for over a year, and when I was twenty, we got the great idea to elope. We didn't have a wedding; we got married on the base at Camp Pendleton in a chapel, and the only people there were officiating the marriage. After we were officially married, I told my foster mother. It wasn't more than a year later that I was pregnant, and then three years later, we had two children. Becoming a mother was one of the most fulfilling experiences of my life. I had the privilege of growing up under the care of a wonderful foster mother who showered me with love and kindness, and I made it my mission to pass on that same kind of love to my children. I was determined never to repeat the mistakes of my birth mother who had been absent and neglectful throughout my childhood. For me, being a mom was a chance to create a better life for my kids and to give them the kind of stable and nurturing home that I had always longed for with my birth mother.

I loved my lifestyle as a mom. I loved being supportive, strong, funny, and being able to be soft but firm all at the same time. I was deeply dedicated to my husband, children, church, and faith. I loved everything that came with all of it. I found joy in being a mother and a wife, attending church services, and following the teachings of God. I was happy, sincerely happy.

I don't know what it is about proclaiming you're happy or in tune with the Lord that stirs up the devil, but I know it does. The devil hates it when we find joy. It seems like whenever you're at the top of your game, loving your life, loving God, and feeling like nothing could take you out, that's the exact moment the devil rears his nasty head. And if the devil can't get to you directly, he will try and get to you through your loved ones.

It was right about this time in my happiness that I noticed a shift in my husband's behavior; to say the least, it wasn't favorable. At first, there were petty arguments that didn't hold much clout. Then his defensive attitude caused him to start an argument for which I was accused of being at fault. After that, he decided to escape by drinking and partying. I would find alcohol bottles, beer cans, and even baggies of drugs around the house. Believe it or not, I remained steadfast by attending church, following God, and praying for us. Despite my efforts to persuade my husband to reevaluate his newfound interests, he continued down a destructive path. He didn't seem to share my passion for being a parent anymore. This caused a massive rift in our relationship. I tried my best to talk to him and help him understand the negative impact of what he was involved with, but he remained indifferent. I felt helpless as I watched him drift further away from me and our family values. He seemed to be now consumed by this lifestyle.

It's not like I thought marriage would always be easy, but I didn't believe it was natural for it to be this difficult. The concerns I was struggling with weren't your average arguments about where the money goes, how to decorate the living room, or whose parents we spent the holidays with. Often, I would come home and see bottles of alcohol, baggies of drugs, beer cans, and masses of people throughout our home. All too frequently, my home looked like a frat house on a Friday night after a baseball game.

As time passed, the situation worsened, and our relationship continued to suffer. I was torn between my love for him and my beliefs. I prayed every night, asking God for guidance and help to heal our marriage. I knew God could fix all this if He wanted to, but nothing seemed to change. How long was I supposed to wait for an answer? When is it okay to give up on your marriage? I knew I was going to have to make a tough decision and, eventually, choose between staying in a toxic relationship or moving on for the sake of my children and my well-being.

My answer came to me one night at 11:45 p.m. I was getting home from work; I walked inside my front door, which was quiet as usual. I walked through my living room and didn't see my husband, so I put down my things and proceeded down the hall to our bedroom. It was at this moment I heard my husband's voice, and as I approached the closed bedroom door, I heard a woman's laugh. When I opened the bedroom door, I found my two daughters sitting on one side of our bed while my husband was on the other side of the bed, holding a glass pipe, bed sheets covering the lower part of his body, and a half-naked woman next to him. If this wasn't a clear and present answer for me, I don't know what would have been. I called my girls over, grabbed them some clothes, and called my foster mother. I left my house that night knowing I was doing the right thing. This needed to happen to give my children a healthy, safe, Christian upbringing.

My foster mother and I had several long talks, and I filed for divorce. I found solace in the company of my foster mother who, once again, proved to be a pillar of support for me. She generously opened her doors to me and my two baby girls and provided us with a safe and comfortable haven to stay in during a difficult time. Her unwavering love, care, and guidance gave me the strength and courage to face my challenges and move forward. I stayed with her for a few months until I found an apartment.

It wasn't always easy moving forward. There were times I didn't feel like getting out of bed; there were times when I wished I could have just turned off my emotions. There were long nights when time seemed to move so slowly that it stopped. My thoughts would overwhelm me. I felt as if I were thinking about everything and nothing all at once. Sometimes, I would reminisce about things that happened in my life, and occasionally, I would ask myself questions about how I ended up here. Perhaps I thought my life would've turned out differently. I've seen the sun rise many times because my mind would not rest. There's a long list of thoughts that would flash through my mind. At these times, I would remember a Bible verse: Psalm 55:22 (KJV), "Cast thy burden upon the LORD, and he shall sustain thee: He shall never suffer the righteous to be moved." This verse has made a tremendous difference in my life.

I've asked God to take my burdens more times than I can count, and He has always sustained me. I wouldn't still be here today if He hadn't. With the good Lord's help, I was able to raise my two children on my own. I returned to college and furthered my education while working two jobs, one of which introduced me to the medical field. I didn't go off and become a doctor, but this field has been a part of my life in everyday circumstances, and I know God introduced me to this for a reason.

I have learned to stay strong and let God handle everything. I have a daily strength with God and the Holy Spirit as my helper. He is with me every step of the way on my journey. I've accepted responsibility for my decisions and am accountable for my actions, just as I am for my mistakes. With God's wisdom, I realized that if I, or anyone else, continued to end up in the same type of displeasing situation and with the same kind of displeasing person, something within us must not be truly healed. When someone is truly healed, the ability to end up in the same situation or with the same type of person won't exist. Your standards will not allow you to settle. Maybe I wasn't completely healed from the trauma of my birth mother before I got married. Come to think of it, I don't remember asking God if that man was the one He blessed for me to marry.

I don't have remorse or any regrets, just more wisdom. I've mastered the art of surviving and want to live a peaceful, godly life. God has made my path smooth since I repented the sin causing me discord. My life is much more peaceful now. I can honestly say that I have been truly healed from the horrors of my childhood and early adult life.

I know most people would find it diffi-cult, or even impossible, to fathom forgiving or letting go of such horrific trauma inflicted by their mother, and they'd be right! On our own, these things are impossible. Only by God's grace can we achieve such unfathomable accomplishments. Even with God's help, some things may take your lifetime to complete, and that's okay. Philippians 1:6 says, "Being confident of this very thing, that he which begun a good work in you will perform *it* until the day of Jesus Christ." God will never give up on the good works He started.

I have seen God take the most broken and impossible situations and restore them. God will take what you think is a mess and create something so beautiful that you look back and say, "Only God could have done this." God had to be working in me because I never thought I'd see the day when I would be around my birth mother by choice, let alone without feeling anxious, bitter, angry, or blaming her for everything I didn't like about my life. God can truly heal the pain of the past no matter what or how your situation may look. It only takes faith and surrendering to the One who holds your life, and you will see how God meets you where you are.

It was less than ten years after I left my husband that my birth mother and I became friends. I was in my thirties when she began to encourage me to be honest, keep words of wisdom close to my heart, and share my knowledge of Christ with others. She told me never to make the same mistakes she made and told me to establish healthy relationships in my life. I immediately thought of the verse from 1 Peter 4:8 that says, "And above all things have fervent charity among yourselves: for charity shall cover the multitude of sins." Thank God for this truth. I'm in awe that I got to witness this word of God taking place as I became friends with my birth mother. What a fantastic experience. Love covered the sin, hurt, and pain I thought I'd carry forever. It doesn't matter what my parents, or your parents for that matter, did or didn't do. You are responsible for the energy you create around you. If you focus on God, His love, and His ways, the energy you create around you will be of the light and good. It's up to you to make that choice. It's not your past relationships, job, economy, or age to blame. It's all part of the journey with God. He gave us free will, and He even gave us a road map to follow. It's up to us to make the right choices.

I stayed in contact with my foster mother throughout my life, and honestly, I consider her to be my mother because she raised me. I was blessed with two mothers, two women of wisdom, and two women of God who will always be a part of me.

It was painful when my birth mother and my foster mother both passed away within one year of each other. That was a lot all at once for me. I'll never forget several things my foster mother told me, but I hold this one dear to my heart, "You are braver than you believe, stronger than you seem, smarter than you think, and loved more than you know." I hold onto this every day. I even see it online in memes and posts, and I think of my foster mother.

My relationship with God is my number one focus. I know that if I care for our relationship, God will care for the rest. I've deepened my relationship with God, and it has deepened my relationship with myself. I am happy being my own best friend. I am pleased with the woman I am today. I've gone through some devastating times while becoming me, and I'm proud of myself who survived. I survived with God's help, and

His rewards are better than I could've ever imagined. I will continue to be my authentic, light-shining self as God intended.

The world can be a dark place at times, but our life in this world is limited. Stop holding onto the things of this world and the things you can't change; let go and let God. Hold onto worshiping God. Put Him first in everything that you do. Find the wonder and amazement in your journey with God. It is truly a blessing. This journey will be my legacy, filled with experiences, both positive and negative, that have contributed to my personal growth. Above all, my relationship with God has been the most significant part of my journey.

If you find yourself struggling, wondering where God is, and feeling alone, I encourage you to believe that there is a purpose for whatever you are facing and that you are not facing it alone. God's plans for us are unchangeable, but we can choose how we respond to them. God said, "For I know the thoughts that I think toward you, saith the Lord, thoughts of peace, and not of evil, to give you an expected end." Resisting won't alter God's plans for you. Accepting the course of events that God has in store can bring peace and understanding. I have submitted my emotions to God, and if you do the same, God will help you manage your journey no matter how painful or difficult it seems.

By surrendering to God, we open our hearts to transformation and guidance on our journey. Humble yourself and commit to Him, allowing Him to shape you into who He intends you to be. I thank God every day for giving me these words to share. God has helped me in many ways, and the Holy Spirit has guided me. Each night, I go to bed smiling, saying, "I am strong; I am enough;

I've made it through another day without giving up, and that's enough for me." Thank you, God.

> For God so loved
> the world, that he gave
> his only begotten Son,
> that whatsoever believeth
> in him should not perish,
> but have everlasting life.
> (John 3:16 KJV)

About the Author

Christine is a devout Christian woman with an unwav-
ering faith in the Bible.
Integrity and honor are an
integral part of her identity.
In a world that is plagued 
by chaos, Christine prioritizes putting God
first in every situation. Growing up as a Creole French Canadian, Christine experienced
firsthand the precipice of racism due to the
color of her skin, despite her mother's Caucasian appearance. In the face of many challenges, Christine has always leaned on God

and allowed Him to guide her through life's hardships. This has been especially useful for overcoming toxic environments and feelings of defeat. Instead of harboring resentment, Christine has embraced her past with clarity and continues to learn from it. She believes that with the help of Jesus, anyone can overcome challenging circumstances and find guidance for their life's journey. Christine wrote this book to inspire people through her story and to help them deepen their relationship with God. She firmly believes that although life is full of ups and downs, Jesus is the best guide to help navigate through them.

www.ingramcontent.com/pod-product-compliance
Lightning Source LLC
Chambersburg PA
CBHW021148130726
47988CB00004B/1519